NELSON'S NEW WEST INDIAN READERS

INFANT BOOK 2

REVISED EDITION

CLIVE BORELY

Illustrated by VAL SANGSTER

OXFORD

UNIVERSITY PRESS

OXFORD
UNIVERSITY PRESS

Great Clarendon Street, Oxford, OX2 6DP, United Kingdom

Oxford University Press is a department of the University of Oxford.
It furthers the University's objective of excellence in research, scholarship,
and education by publishing worldwide. Oxford is a registered trade mark of
Oxford University Press in the UK and in certain other countries

Text © Clive Borely 1973, 1987
Original illustrations © Oxford University Press 2015

The moral rights of the authors have been asserted

First published by Thomas Nelson and Sons Ltd in 1973
Second edition published by Thomas Nelson and Sons Ltd in 1987
This edition published by Oxford University Press in 2015

British Library Cataloguing in Publication Data
Data available

978-0-1756-6344-6

20 19 18 17 16

Printed in India by Multivista Global Pvt. Ltd.

Acknowledgements
Illustrations: Val Sangster

Although we have made every effort to trace and contact all
copyright holders before publication this has not been possible in all
cases. If notified, the publisher will rectify any errors or omissions at
the earliest opportunity.

Links to third party websites are provided by Oxford in good faith
and for information only. Oxford disclaims any responsibility for
the materials contained in any third party website referenced in
this work.

TO THE TEACHER

This book is a continuation of Infant Book 1.
It continues to teach the child the phonic
principles started in Book 1, and new
words that obey the rules already learnt
should be "worked out" by the child, not
learnt by sight as whole words. It is only by
practice that the skills being taught will be
mastered.

It is through the sentence that the ideas
of the writer are conveyed to the reader.
Sentences should be read as meaningful
units, with the appropriate phrasing and
intonation. Incomprehensible muttering
and halting word-by-word reading must be
discouraged from the start. It might be
necessary for a child to work through a
sentence slowly, word by word, at the start,
but when all the words are recognised, the
sentence should be re-read properly
before passing on to the next.

Non-phonic words have to be taught as
"sight words". Sufficient practice in word
recognition of this kind must be given to
ensure the immediate understanding of
these words.

C.B.

K

k

W

w

V

v

Y

y

J

j

I

band	fall	can	bell	bet	ham
hand	wall	fan	fell	yet	jam
sand	ball	van	well	vet	Sam
wand	call	man	yell	set	yam
	tall		Nell	get	
				let	

Here comes the big red van.

"Come, Ann. Get me some jam from
the van."

Sam and Ann ran to the van.

The old man in the van sold Ann the jam.

"I have some jam. Do you want jam?"

"Oh yes, we want jam."

Sam and Ann took the jam and ran
to the hut.

2

Sam ran to the wall.
"I can hop on the wall.
I am tall, the king of the wall."
"No, don't hop on the wall. You will fall."
Poor king tall fell from the wall.
The jam fell from his hand.

"Come, Mummy. Sam fell from the wall."
Mummy ran to Sam.
Mummy is mad. Sam is sad.
He cut his hand. He has no jam.
"Poor Sam," said Mummy. "Don't cry.
Let me kiss you."

Th   th

Ch   ch

Sh   sh

thin	chat	shall
thing	chap	shell
thumb	chip	ship
think	chop	shop

Dad went to the shop with Sam.
"What do you want, Sam?
Tell me what you want most of all."
"I want a lot of things.
But I think I want the ship most of all."
"Well, I shall get the ship for you."
"Boy! Now I can sail my ship
    when we go to the sea."

look	sing	duck	pay
cook	ring	luck	say
book	sang	sack	way
took	rang	pack	day

Ann likes to help her mother cook.
She wants to be a good cook one day.
She got the cook-book and went to mother.
"Look, Mummy, I want to make a
    cake. Let us make a cake."
"Good. I shall help you.
    One day you will make a cake and I
      shall cook a duck.
    If the sun shines, we shall have a picnic."
"Boy!" said Ann, "that will be fun."

Ann likes cake. She made a cake.
There is a cake sale today at the church.
Ann made a cake for the sale.
Mother helped her make the cake.
Ann will be a good cook.
She likes to cook and bake.

mad	made	Sam	same	nice
at	ate	man	mane	mice
rid	ride	not	note	like
Tim	time	hop	hope	Mike
hid	hide	us	use	bike
kit	kite	tub	tube	nine

Mike has five pets. He has a dog,
   a cat, and three rabbits.
Mike says that his cat has nine lives.
It is a nice cat.
It plays with Mike's ball. It does not
   like mice.
Mummy is glad for that. The cat has
   got rid of all the mice in the house.

cry   dry   fry   try   fly

One day Mike made a kite.
It was a big, red kite. He put the kite
on the bed and went to call Sam.
"Come, Sam, let's go and fly the kite."
"Sorry, Mike," said Sam. "Not this
time. I have to stay home and do
my home work."
"O.K., Sam. I will go and hide the kite.
I hope we can fly it some other time.
We have to try to fly it on a dry, windy day."

Jane	June	same	note
cane	tune	game	pole
lane		tame	hole
		lame	

Jane sings a song about the moon in June.
It has a nice tune.
Ann and Sam hum the tune all the time.
Dad does not like the tune.
He says all the songs are the same.
He does not sing at all. He cannot sing a note.

Ann and Jane play a little game.
Ann hums a tune and Jane has to try
    to give the name of the tune.
If she gets the name of the song it is
    her turn to hum a tune.
Ann hums, "Jane and Louisa will
    soon come home."
Jane says the name. Then Jane and
    Ann sing the song together.

meet	beat	meal
teeth	team	seal
feet	meat	deal
seem	seat	heal
feel	feat	beach

One day Dad took David and Ann to
  the beach.
  They went by bus.
"Let me pay the fare," said Ann.
"Here is the beach," said Dad.
"May I go into the sea, Dad?" said Ann.
"May I go too?" said David.
"Wait for me!" said Dad.

Tim and John were on a seat on the beach.
Ann and David ran to meet them.
They ran and played on the sand.
They liked to feel the sand under their feet.

"Teach me to swim, Dad," said David.
"Me too," said Ann.
   Dad took them into the sea.
   They liked the sea a lot.

"Come, let's eat," called Dad.
  They went to the seat and ate bread
    and meat.
  They had a sweet drink.
"It's time to go now," said Dad.
"No. Let's stay a little more," said David.
"Come on. We have to leave now.
  We'll come back some day soon."

boat	bow	few
coat	sow	new
goat	low	dew
load	row	mew

Mr Hoad has a new boat.
Tim and David went to see the boat.
"Boy! It is a big boat. I'll bet it is a
    fast boat.
It can beat any boat in a race."

"Oh no!" said Mr Hoad. "It's not a
    fast boat."
"Is it a slow boat?"
"Is it a row boat?"
"I want to row the boat, Mr Hoad."
  Mr Hoad smiled.
"We don't have to row, David.
    We have an engine."

"When we take it down to the sea
    I'll take you for a ride."
"Boy! Can Ann come too?"
"Yes, we can take a few more.
    But only a few."
"Thank you, Mr Hoad."
    David and Tim ran down the road to
        tell Mohan and Sita.

blow	glass	play	slow
black	glad	plot	slap
bless	glum	plan	slim

21

All the boys and girls hear about
Mr Hoad's boat.
They are glad for Mr Hoad. He is a
fisherman but his old boat was lost at sea.
He could not go out to fish.
He kept a few goats and sold milk
and goat meat.
Now he has his new boat he can fish again.

Mr Hoad will put his boat in the water today.
John, David and Tim have to come to help.
They will push the boat into the water.
A lot of Mr Hoad's friends come too.
They push and push. The boat is big
   and heavy.
It goes slowly. At last it is in the water.
They are all glad.

"Can we go for a ride?" asked Tim.
"Oh, yes," said Mr Hoad. "Come in."
  Mr Hoad took the boys for a ride
    around the bay.
  Then he told them, "I have to take you
    back now. I have to go fishing. I'll take
    you for a long ride another day."
"Thank you, Mr Hoad," said the boys
    as they ran up the beach.

brush	grow	free	tram
broom	grass	front	trap
branch	grape	fresh	trot

Joan and Sita live in the country.
They like it.
They have lots of trees in their yard.
The grass in front of the house is cut low.
They like to run and play on the grass.
In the back they have fruit trees.
The trees grow well in the country.
Joan and Sita can climb. They like
    fresh fruit. They climb the trees and
    pick the fruits.

There is a coconut tree, too.
The coconut tree grows very tall.
Joan and Sita cannot climb it. It is too tall.
They make brooms from the leaves of
    the coconut tree.
They keep the yard clean with the
    coconut brooms.

There is a donkey on the farm.
John tried to hold it.
It trotted away. When he gets near
    it trots away.
"I will trap him," said John. "I'll get
    him into the back of the yard and
    tie him to the tree."
But the donkey ran into the field.
He wanted to be free.

boy	noise	born	farm
toy	coin	torn	harm
joy	soil	worn	hard
	boil	corn	yard

Sita and Tim like the country.
They like to go to their uncle's farm.
On the farm he keeps pigs, cows
    and chickens.
He also plants corn in the back yard.
Today all the children came to see
    the farm.
They think it's all fun.
But Uncle Paul has to work hard.

The boys wanted to ride the donkey.

"No," said Uncle Paul.

"When you are a little older."

Just then they heard a loud noise.

They all jumped.

Uncle Paul smiled.

"It's only the donkey. That's how he goes."

"I thought he went 'hee haw'," said Tim.

"It is a little like 'hee haw', but it's
        much louder."

The girls went with Aunt Zena to pick corn.
"We are going to boil the corn," said Sita.
"Boy! Boiled corn! I like that.
  When I get big I'll have a farm and
    eat boiled corn all day," said Tim.
  Uncle Paul laughed.
"No, you won't," he said. "A farmer
    has to work hard and dig the soil
    before he can reap his crop. You
    take life too easily to be a farmer."

cage	judge	rice	grace
rage	fudge	mice	place
stage	wedge	nice	space
edge	hedge	spice	fence

Our little friends went to the Zoo.
Aunt Zena gave them money to buy
 sweets.
They went to see the lion first.
He was in a big cage. The lion sat on
 a stage at the back of the cage.
Tim wanted the lion to stand up.
He went to the edge of the cage.
"Come back here!" called Jane.
Tim came back.

They went to see the monkeys.
They were jumping up and down and
hanging by their tails.
Sita threw a nut for one. He picked it
up and ate it.
Then all the children threw sweets.
John gave one his fudge.
Tim gave one a rice cake. Jane gave
one an ice-cream cone.
"Don't give the monkeys all your
sweets," said an old man.
"Eat some yourselves."

"Look at the deer and the wild hog,"
    said John.
  They ran up to the fence. The deer
    came up to the fence and put his
    nose through a hole.
  John gave it a nut. It turned and ran
    back to its place under a tree.

air	care	bird	turn
pair	dare	firm	fur
stair	stare		burn
fair			

The girls like the birds best.
"They are so pretty," said Joan.
"Look at that pair of swans on the lake.
See how graceful they are.
I like the little baby swans.
I wish I could take them home."
"That's not fair. They will miss
their mummy.
In any case you don't have a pond
for them to swim on."

It was time to go. They all had to
go home.
"I like the bear best. It has nice fur."
"I don't like the lion. He just sits and stares
at us. I can beat that old lion," said Tim.
"I can go into his cage and give him
one hard blow on his head."

"Oh, no you can't. You don't dare do that."
"Oh, yes I can," said Tim. "He is a silly
old lion. All he does is sleep all day."
"He's not silly. He's tame, but he can
eat you all up."

"I don't care what you say. I can beat that old lion."
R..O..A..R! went the lion.
Tim jumped and started to run.
All the children laughed at him.

box   queen   zebra
fox   quick   zip
           quite   zoo

Once upon a time, in a country
    far away there lived a queen.
Her name was Queen Zola.
Zola wanted all the children in her
    land to have a treat.
She told her Prime Minister to call in
    a circus.
Soon the circus came.
There were lions and tigers
    and elephants with long tusks
    and huge ears like fans.

There were zebras with their long
    black stripes.
There were apes and chimpanzees.
There was also a red fox in a big box.
There were clowns that made the
    children laugh.
There were acrobats who made them
    sit and wonder.
At the end of the show the children
    were all very happy.

Word List

B	C	D	F	G	H	J	L	M
babe	cage	dame	face	gold	hate	jade	lake	made
bake	came	dane	fade	game	hail	Jake	lame	make
bale	cane	date	fake	gate	hay	Jane	late	mane
bare	cape	Dave	fame	gave	hard	jail	laid	mate
bail	case	daze	fate	gaze	harm	jar	lain	maze
bait	cave	dark	fail	gain	harp		lay	maid
bay	coil	darn	foil	gay	hoop		lard	may
bar	coin	dart	feed	glad			lord	
bark	car		feel	glass			look	
barn	card		far	globe				
born	Carl		farm	glum				
book	corn		fair	glow	N	P	Q
boot	cook		flag	glue	name	page	queen
bow	cool		flat	grab	nine	pale	queer
buck	code		fled	grass		pane	quick
bug	coke		flew	grace		paid	quite
bun	cone		flit	green		pail	
	chap		flip	grew		pain	
	chat		flick	grip		pay	
	chess		flog	grow		pair	
	chart		flock			plan	
	chum		flop			play	
	chew		flow			place	
			flute			plow	
			fret			plum	
			frog			pram	
			frock			pray	

R	S	T	V	W	Y			
rage	sake	take	van	wage	yam	grace	air	and
rate	sale	tale	vest	wait	yard	place	fair	band
rave	same	tame	vent	way	yes	space	pair	hand
raid	save	tape	veal	west	yet	trace	hair	land
rail	sail	tail	vote	went	yell		stair	sand
rain	say	toil		well				stand
ray	soil	toy		will				grand
rent	shack	took		win				
rest	shed	track		wait		all	budge	
rust	shell	tram		week		ball	fudge	
	ship	trap		weed		fall	judge	
	sheep	train		what		hall	nudge	
	sheet	trace		when		mall		
	slack	true		where		tall		
	slam	trail		which		wall		
	slap	trick		why		stall		
	sleep	trip		who		small		
	slept							
	slot				Z	oar	boat	
	slow				zap	boar	coat	
	stall				zip	roar	goat	
	star				zig-zag	soar		
	stay							
	stem							
	stick							
	still							
	stop							